MY ESTATE PLANNER

Essential Information for My Family

A Record Book of My Documents, Assets & Obligations

MY ESTATE PLANNER

Essential Information for My Family

A Record Book of My
Documents, Assets & Obligations

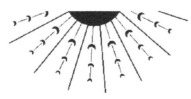

SUNSHINE PUBLICATIONS

MY PERSONAL INFORMATION

Legal Name _____

Maiden Name _____

Address _____

Address _____

City _____ State _____ Country _____

Telephone 1 _____ Password _____

Telephone 2 _____ Password _____

Emergency Contact _____

Telephone _____

Social Security # _____

Driver License # _____

Email 1 _____

Email 2 _____

Computer 1 Password _____

Computer 2 Password _____

Tablet 1 Password _____ Tablet 2 Password _____

Watch Password _____ eReader Password _____

Primary Care Physician _____

Telephone _____ Email _____

Dentist _____

Telephone _____ Email _____

Preferred Hospital _____

Address _____

Telephone _____

Local Pharmacy_____ Telephone_____

Birthplace _____

Marital Status _____

Spouse's Name _____

Former Spouse's Name _____

My Children's Names _____

_____

_____

My Sibling's Name _____

_____

_____

My Mother's Name/Maiden Name _____

My Father's Name _____

Medical Conditions _____

_____

_____

Medications _____

_____

_____

_____

HOW TO USE YOUR PLANNER

A *Sunshine Publications **suggested*** usage of your easy-to-use interactive personal Planner. Of course, you determine how it can be most valuable and beneficial to you and your loved ones.

1. Purchase or receive as a gift your new Sunshine Publications *My Estate Planner (Essential Information for My Family).*

2. Fill in the blanks of as many categories of the comprehensive "Table of Contents" as is most useful to you and your family. You may not need to complete the entire planner.

3. Keep your planner in an accessible but secure place!

4. Entrust the location of your completed planner to your most trusted relative, friend or legal representative, so someone will have access to your most trusted information when it is most needed.

5. Due to changes in personal and business information, we **suggest** that you update your planner at least once per year.

Now you can rest assured that your loved ones will be spared the confusion, stress and anxiety of the hunt and gathering of your well-lived life's information, documents and obligations. Remember, many accounts of all kinds, including social media, will have to be located and closed. This peace-of-mind planner makes this daunting, sometimes overwhelming task, much easier during loss, severe illness or incapacitation. The information is right here, all in one secure place.

You do not have to share your personal information with anyone, simply share the LOCATION of, My Estate Planner with one person, one family member, a best friend, a legal representative. Your person...

Don't forget *My Estate Planner (Essential Information for My Family)* is available in paperback, hardcover and an ultra-easy PDF interactive download *ePlanner* version at:

www.SunshinePublicationsLLC.com

Published by:
Sunshine Publications LLC
7004 Kennedy Boulevard East - Suite 11f Guttenberg,
NJ 07093 USA

My Estate Planner (Information for My Family)
Copyright © 1989 by Marion J. Caffey
First printing December 1989
Printed in the United States of America
Library of Congress Cataloging in Publication Data
Library of Congress Catalog Card Number 89-92062
Caffey, Marion J. 1955 -
"My Estate Planner" (Information for My Family)

My Estate Planner (Essential Information for My Family)
Copyright © 2022 by Marion J. Caffey
First printing April 2022
Printed in the United States of America

ISBN: 978-0-578-37160-3

TABLE OF CONTENTS

THE IMPORTANCE OF A LAST WILL AND TESTAMENT

The information contained in this book will be of untold value and assistance to you, your family, personal and legal representatives. However, *it will not*, determine the disposition of your assets or property in the event of your death. Only your *Last Will and Testament* can do that. If you do not have a will at the present time, we encourage you to consult an attorney or legal representative and arrange to execute one as soon as possible. *My Estate Planner* is not a legal document, nor does it intend to replace any legal documents.

My Estate Planner is a valuable record book to give you, your family and representatives locations of your legal and common documents, assets, information, and obligations for total peace of mind during the most difficult of times.

# WILLS & TRUSTS

I have a *Last Will and Testament*, which was executed on

_____

and is located at _____

In care of _____

Executor information _____

_____

I have a *Living Will*, which was executed on

_____

Location _____

In care of _____

Executor information _____

_____

I have a *Revocable Trust*, which was executed on

_____

Location _____

In care of _____

Executor information _____

_____

I have an *Irrevocable Trust*, which was executed on

_____

Location _____

In care of _____

Executor information _____

_____

IMPORTANT DOCUMENT LOCATION
❖ QUICK GUIDE ❖
(Where Did I Put My...)

We have provided a quick & easy guide for you to specify the locations of your most important documents. Simply enter the letter code (shown in parentheses) in the *LOCATION TABLE* (below), into the underlined space next to the appropriate document in the *DOCUMENT TABLE* (to your right). An easy way for you to remember or your loved ones to easily discover, the locations of your most important and valuable documents.

Keep this easily accessible to you to use on an as-needed basis. Also, it will be of untold value to your loved ones at the time they will need information and comfort the most.

LOCATION TABLE
(Where I Keep My Things)

(A) Attorney	(M) Mother
(AU) Automobile (Glove Box)	(O) Office
(B) Bank	(P) Partner
(BF) Brokerage Firm	(PU) Purse
(BR) Brother	(R) Relative
(C) Computer	(RB) Real Estate Broker
(CL) In my Closet	(RC) Religious Counselor
(D) Daughter	(SC) Spiritual Counselor
(DB) Safe Deposit Box	(S) Son
(F) Father	(SP) Spouse
(FC) File Cabinet (Home)	(ST) Sister
(FP) Financial Planner	(T) Smart Phone
(FN) Friend	(UM) Under my Mattress
(FD) Funeral Director	(V) Vehicle
(HO) Home Office	(W) Wallet
(HS) Home Safe	(WD) Work Desk

DOCUMENT TABLE
(My Important Things)

_____Artwork Certification

_____Adoption Information

_____Automobile Title(s)

_____Birth Certificate

_____Burial Information

_____Businesses Info.

_____Cash

_____Child Custody Records

_____Citizenship Records

_____Computer Passcode

_____Cremation Certificate

_____Crypto Keys

_____Death Certificate(s)

_____Deed(s)

_____Divorce Information

_____Home Rental Contract

_____Income Tax Returns

_____Interment Certificate

_____Marriage Certificate(s)

_____Military Discharge

_____Mortgage Information

_____NFT Key(s)

_____Nursing Home Contract

_____Passport(s)

_____Pension Information

_____Property Deed(s)

_____Rare Coins

_____Retirement Info.

_____Safe Deposit Keys

_____Social Security Card

_____Other_____

_____Other_____

_____Other_____

Insurance Policies

_____Auto

_____Boat

_____Business

_____Health

_____Home

_____Life

_____Jewelry

_____Pet

_____Renters

_____Other Vehicles

_____Other_____

_____Other_____

ANNUITIES

Financial Institution _____

Address _____

Representative _____

Website _____

Telephone _____ Email _____

Account No. _____

Certificate Length _____ Maturity Date _____

Annuity Amount _____

Payment Frequency _____

Financial Institution _____

Address _____

Representative _____

Website _____

Telephone _____ Email _____

Account No. _____

Certificate Length _____ Maturity Date _____

Annuity Amount _____

Payment Frequency _____

ANNUITIES

Financial Institution _____

Address _____

Representative _____

Website _____

Telephone _____ Email _____

Account No. _____

Certificate Length _____ Maturity Date _____

Annuity Amount _____

Payment Frequency _____

Financial Institution _____

Address _____

Representative _____

Website _____

Telephone _____ Email _____

Account No. _____

Certificate Length _____ Maturity Date _____

Annuity Amount _____

Payment Frequency _____

Financial Institution _____

Address _____

Representative _____

Website _____

Telephone _____ Email _____

Account No. _____

Certificate Length _____ Maturity Date _____

Annuity Amount _____

Payment Frequency _____

ANNUITIES

Financial Institution _____

Address _____

Representative _____

Website _____

Telephone _____ Email _____

Account No. _____

Certificate Length _____ Maturity Date _____

Annuity Amount _____

Payment Frequency _____

Financial Institution _____

Address _____

Representative _____

Website _____

Telephone _____ Email _____

Account No. _____

Certificate Length _____ Maturity Date _____

Annuity Amount _____

Payment Frequency _____

Financial Institution _____

Address _____

Representative _____

Website _____

Telephone _____ Email _____

Account No. _____

Certificate Length _____ Maturity Date _____

Annuity Amount _____

Payment Frequency _____

ANNUITIES

Financial Institution _____

Address _____

Representative _____

Website _____

Telephone _____ Email _____

Account No. _____

Certificate Length _____ Maturity Date _____

Annuity Amount _____

Payment Frequency _____

Financial Institution _____

Address _____

Representative _____

Website _____

Telephone _____ Email _____

Account No. _____

Certificate Length _____ Maturity Date _____

Annuity Amount _____

Payment Frequency _____

Financial Institution _____

Address _____

Representative _____

Website _____

Telephone _____ Email _____

Account No. _____

Certificate Length _____ Maturity Date _____

Annuity Amount _____

Payment Frequency _____

BANK ✦ CREDIT UNION ✦ SAVINGS & LOAN
(Checking, Savings, Money Market, Other..........)

Financial Institution _____

Account Type _____

Address _____

Website _____

Account No. _____

Telephone _____ Email _____

Personal Contact _____

Notes _____

Financial Institution _____

Account Type _____

Address _____

Website _____

Account No. _____

Telephone _____ Email _____

Personal Contact _____

Notes _____

BANK ♦ CREDIT UNION ♦ SAVINGS & LOAN
(Checking, Savings, Money Market, Other...........)

Financial Institution ———————————————————

Account Type ———————————————————

Address ———————————————————

Website ———————————————————

Account No. ———————————————————

Telephone ——————————— Email ———————————

Personal Contact ———————————————————

Notes ———————————————————

Financial Institution ———————————————————

Account Type ———————————————————

Address ———————————————————

Website ———————————————————

Account No. ———————————————————

Telephone ——————————— Email ———————————

Personal Contact ———————————————————

Notes ———————————————————

Financial Institution ———————————————————

Account Type ———————————————————

Address ———————————————————

Website ———————————————————

Account No. ———————————————————

Telephone ——————————— Email ———————————

Personal Contact ———————————————————

Notes ———————————————————

BROKERAGE ✦ RETIREMENT ACCOUNTS
(401K, Stocks, Bonds, ETF, Futures, IRA, Options, SEP, Treasuries, Commodities...)

Financial Institution _____

Account Type _____

Associated Business/Employer _____

Address _____

Address _____

Security _____ Shares _____

Security _____ Shares _____

Security _____ Shares _____

Security _____ Shares _____

Commodity _____ Commodity _____

Website _____

Account _____

Telephone _____ Email _____

Personal Contact _____

Notes _____

BROKERAGE ♦ RETIREMENT ACCOUNTS

Financial Institution _____

Account Type _____

Associated Business/Employer _____

Address _____

Address _____

Security _____ Shares _____

Security _____ Shares _____

Security _____ Shares _____

Security _____ Shares _____

Commodity _____ Commodity _____

Website _____

Account _____

Telephone _____ Email _____

Personal Contact _____

Notes _____

Financial Institution _____

Account Type _____

Associated Business/Employer _____

Address _____

Address _____

Security _____ Shares _____

Security _____ Shares _____

Security _____ Shares _____

Security _____ Shares _____

Commodity _____ Commodity _____

Website _____

Account _____

Telephone _____ Email _____

Personal Contact _____

Notes _____

BROKERAGE ♦ RETIREMENT ACCOUNTS

Financial Institution _____

Account Type _____

Associated Business/Employer _____

Address _____

Address _____

Security _____ Shares _____

Security _____ Shares _____

Security _____ Shares _____

Security _____ Shares _____

Commodity _____ Commodity _____

Website _____

Account _____

Telephone _____ Email _____

Personal Contact _____

Notes _____

Financial Institution _____

Account Type _____

Associated Business/Employer _____

Address _____

Address _____

Security _____ Shares _____

Security _____ Shares _____

Security _____ Shares _____

Security _____ Shares _____

Commodity _____ Commodity _____

Website _____

Account _____

Telephone _____ Email _____

Personal Contact _____

Notes _____

BROKERAGE ♦ RETIREMENT ACCOUNTS

Financial Institution _____

Account Type _____

Associated Business/Employer _____

Address _____

Address _____

Security _____ Shares _____

Security _____ Shares _____

Security _____ Shares _____

Security _____ Shares _____

Commodity _____ Commodity _____

Website _____

Account _____

Telephone _____ Email _____

Personal Contact _____

Notes _____

Financial Institution _____

Account Type _____

Associated Business/Employer _____

Address _____

Address _____

Security _____ Shares _____

Security _____ Shares _____

Security _____ Shares _____

Security _____ Shares _____

Commodity _____ Commodity _____

Website _____

Account _____

Telephone _____ Email _____

Personal Contact _____

Notes _____

BROKERAGE ✦ RETIREMENT ACCOUNTS

Financial Institution _____

Account Type _____

Associated Business/Employer _____

Address _____

Address _____

Security _____ Shares _____

Security _____ Shares _____

Security _____ Shares _____

Security _____ Shares _____

Commodity _____ Commodity _____

Website _____

Account _____

Telephone _____ Email _____

Personal Contact _____

Notes _____

Financial Institution _____

Account Type _____

Associated Business/Employer _____

Address _____

Address _____

Security _____ Shares _____

Security _____ Shares _____

Security _____ Shares _____

Security _____ Shares _____

Commodity _____ Commodity _____

Website _____

Account _____

Telephone _____ Email _____

Personal Contact _____

Notes _____

BROKERAGE ◆ RETIREMENT ACCOUNTS

Financial Institution _____

Account Type _____

Associated Business/Employer _____

Address _____

Address _____

Security _____ Shares _____

Security _____ Shares _____

Security _____ Shares _____

Security _____ Shares _____

Commodity _____ Commodity _____

Website _____

Account _____

Telephone _____ Email _____

Personal Contact _____

Notes _____

Financial Institution _____

Account Type _____

Associated Business/Employer _____

Address _____

Address _____

Security _____ Shares _____

Security _____ Shares _____

Security _____ Shares _____

Security _____ Shares _____

Commodity _____ Commodity _____

Website _____

Account _____

Telephone _____ Email _____

Personal Contact _____

Notes _____

BUSINESS ✦ EMPLOYMENT

Name of Business _____

Address _____

Address _____

City _____ State _____ Zip Code _____

Country _____

Principals _____

My Position ☐ Owner ☐ Partner ☐ Employee ☐ Consultant

Supervisor _____

Telephone _____ Email _____

Length of Service _____ Since _____

Salary $ _____ Fee $ _____

Stock Option ☐ Yes ☐ No   Pension Benefit ☐ Yes ☐ No

Ins. Benefits ☐ Yes ☐ No   SS Benefits ☐ Yes ☐ No

Other Benefits _____

Notes _____

BUSINESS ♦ EMPLOYMENT

Name of Business _____

Address _____

Address _____

City _____ State _____ Zip Code _____

Country _____

Principals _____

My Position ☐ Owner ☐ Partner ☐ Employee ☐ Consultant

Supervisor _____

Telephone _____ Email _____

Length of Service _____ Since _____

Salary $ _____ Fee $ _____

Stock Option ☐ Yes ☐ No   Pension Benefit ☐ Yes ☐ No

Ins. Benefits ☐ Yes ☐ No   SS Benefits ☐ Yes ☐ No

Other Benefits _____

Notes _____

Name of Business _____

Address _____

Address _____

City _____ State _____ Zip Code _____

Country _____

Principals _____

My Position ☐ Owner ☐ Partner ☐ Employee ☐ Consultant

Supervisor _____

Telephone _____ Email _____

Length of Service _____ Since _____

Salary $ _____ Fee $ _____

Stock Option ☐ Yes ☐ No   Pension Benefit ☐ Yes ☐ No

Ins. Benefits ☐ Yes ☐ No   SS Benefits ☐ Yes ☐ No

Other Benefits _____

Notes _____

BUSINESS ♦ EMPLOYMENT

Name of Business _____

Address _____

Address _____

City _____ State _____ Zip Code _____

Country _____

Principals _____

My Position ☐ Owner ☐ Partner ☐ Employee ☐ Consultant

Supervisor _____

Telephone _____ Email _____

Length of Service _____ Since _____

Salary $ _____ Fee $ _____

Stock Option ☐ Yes ☐ No   Pension Benefit ☐ Yes ☐ No

Ins. Benefits ☐ Yes ☐ No   SS Benefits ☐ Yes ☐ No

Other Benefits _____

Notes _____

Name of Business _____

Address _____

Address _____

City _____ State _____ Zip Code _____

Country _____

Principals _____

My Position ☐ Owner ☐ Partner ☐ Employee ☐ Consultant

Supervisor _____

Telephone _____ Email _____

Length of Service _____ Since _____

Salary $ _____ Fee $ _____

Stock Option ☐ Yes ☐ No   Pension Benefit ☐ Yes ☐ No

Ins. Benefits ☐ Yes ☐ No   SS Benefits ☐ Yes ☐ No

Other Benefits _____

Notes _____

BUSINESS ♦ EMPLOYMENT

Name of Business _____

Address _____

Address _____

City _____ State _____ Zip Code _____

Country _____

Principals _____

My Position ☐ Owner ☐ Partner ☐ Employee ☐ Consultant

Supervisor _____

Telephone _____ Email _____

Length of Service _____ Since _____

Salary $ _____ Fee $ _____

Stock Option ☐ Yes ☐ No   Pension Benefit ☐ Yes ☐ No

Ins. Benefits ☐ Yes ☐ No   SS Benefits ☐ Yes ☐ No

Other Benefits _____

Notes _____

Name of Business _____

Address _____

Address _____

City _____ State _____ Zip Code _____

Country _____

Principals _____

My Position ☐ Owner ☐ Partner ☐ Employee ☐ Consultant

Supervisor _____

Telephone _____ Email _____

Length of Service _____ Since _____

Salary $ _____ Fee $ _____

Stock Option ☐ Yes ☐ No   Pension Benefit ☐ Yes ☐ No

Ins. Benefits ☐ Yes ☐ No   SS Benefits ☐ Yes ☐ No

Other Benefits _____

Notes _____

CERTIFICATE OF DEPOSIT

Financial Institution _____

Address _____

Website _____

Telephone _____ Email _____

Account No. _____

Certificate No. _____

Certificate Length _____ Maturity Date _____

Certificate Amount _____

Certificate Interest Rate _____

Financial Institution _____

Address _____

Website _____

Telephone _____ Email _____

Account No. _____

Certificate No. _____

Certificate Length _____ Maturity Date _____

Certificate Amount _____

Certificate Interest Rate _____

CERTIFICATE OF DEPOSIT

Financial Institution _____

Address _____

Website _____

Telephone _____ Email _____

Account No. _____

Certificate No. _____

Certificate Length _____ Maturity Date _____

Certificate Amount _____

Certificate Interest Rate _____

Financial Institution _____

Address _____

Website _____

Telephone _____ Email _____

Account No. _____

Certificate No. _____

Certificate Length _____ Maturity Date _____

Certificate Amount _____

Certificate Interest Rate _____

Financial Institution _____

Address _____

Website _____

Telephone _____ Email _____

Account No. _____

Certificate No. _____

Certificate Length _____ Maturity Date _____

Certificate Amount _____

Certificate Interest Rate _____

CERTIFICATE OF DEPOSIT

Financial Institution _____

Address _____

Website _____

Telephone _____ Email _____

Account No. _____

Certificate No. _____

Certificate Length _____ Maturity Date _____

Certificate Amount _____

Certificate Interest Rate _____

Financial Institution _____

Address _____

Website _____

Telephone _____ Email _____

Account No. _____

Certificate No. _____

Certificate Length _____ Maturity Date _____

Certificate Amount _____

Certificate Interest Rate _____

Financial Institution _____

Address _____

Website _____

Telephone _____ Email _____

Account No. _____

Certificate No: _____

Certificate Length _____ Maturity Date _____

Certificate Amount _____

Certificate Interest Rate _____

CERTIFICATE OF DEPOSIT

Financial Institution _____

Address _____

Website _____

Telephone _____ Email _____

Account No. _____

Certificate No. _____

Certificate Length _____ Maturity Date _____

Certificate Amount _____

Certificate Interest Rate _____

Financial Institution _____

Address _____

Website _____

Telephone _____ Email _____

Account No. _____

Certificate No. _____

Certificate Length _____ Maturity Date _____

Certificate Amount _____

Certificate Interest Rate _____

Financial Institution _____

Address _____

Website _____

Telephone _____ Email _____

Account No. _____

Certificate No. _____

Certificate Length _____ Maturity Date _____

Certificate Amount _____

Certificate Interest Rate _____

CREDIT ✦ CHARGE ✦ DEBIT ✦
ELECTRONIC PAYMENT

(AMEX, Apple Pay, Bank of America, Cash App, Chase, Discover, Google Pay, Mastercard, PayPal, Square, Venmo, Visa, Walmart, Wells Fargo, Zelle, Other...)

Financial Institution _____

Card Type _____

Address _____

Associated Company _____

Website _____

Account No. _____

Card No. _____

Telephone _____ Email _____

Personal Contact _____

Balance $ _____ Monthly Payment $ _____

Notes _____

CREDIT ♦ CHARGE ♦ DEBIT ♦ ELECTRONIC PAYMENT

(AMEX, Apple Pay, Bank of America, Cash App, Chase, Discover, Google Pay, Mastercard, PayPal, Square, Venmo, Visa, Walmart, Wells Fargo, Zelle, Other...)

Financial Institution _____

Card Type _____

Address _____

Associated Company _____

Website _____

Account No. _____

Card No. _____

Telephone _____ Email _____

Personal Contact _____

Balance $ _____ Monthly Payment $ _____

Notes _____

Financial Institution _____

Card Type _____

Address _____

Associated Company _____

Website _____

Account No. _____

Card No. _____

Telephone _____ Email _____

Personal Contact _____

Balance $ _____ Monthly Payment $ _____

Notes _____

CREDIT ♦ CHARGE ♦ DEBIT ♦ ELECTRONIC PAYMENT

(AMEX, Apple Pay, Bank of America, Cash App, Chase, Discover, Google Pay, Mastercard, PayPal, Square, Venmo, Visa, Walmart, Wells Fargo, Zelle, Other...)

Financial Institution _____

Card Type _____

Address _____

Associated Company _____

Website _____

Account No. _____

Card No. _____

Telephone _____ Email _____

Personal Contact _____

Balance $ _____ Monthly Payment $ _____

Notes _____

Financial Institution _____

Card Type _____

Address _____

Associated Company _____

Website _____

Account No. _____

Card No. _____

Telephone _____ Email _____

Personal Contact _____

Balance $ _____ Monthly Payment $ _____

Notes _____

CREDIT ♦ CHARGE ♦ DEBIT ♦ ELECTRONIC PAYMENT

(AMEX, Apple Pay, Bank of America, Cash App, Chase, Discover, Google Pay, Mastercard, PayPal, Square, Venmo, Visa, Walmart, Wells Fargo, Zelle, Other...)

Financial Institution _____

Card Type _____

Address _____

Associated Company _____

Website _____

Account No. _____

Card No. _____

Telephone _____ Email _____

Personal Contact _____

Balance $ _____ Monthly Payment $ _____

Notes _____

Financial Institution _____

Card Type _____

Address _____

Associated Company _____

Website _____

Account No. _____

Card No. _____

Telephone _____ Email _____

Personal Contact _____

Balance $ _____ Monthly Payment $ _____

Notes _____

CREDIT ♦ CHARGE ♦ DEBIT ♦ ELECTRONIC PAYMENT

(AMEX, Apple Pay, Bank of America, Cash App, Chase, Discover, Google Pay, Mastercard, PayPal, Square, Venmo, Visa, Walmart, Wells Fargo, Zelle, Other...)

Financial Institution _____

Card Type _____

Address _____

Associated Company _____

Website _____

Account No. _____

Card No. _____

Telephone _____ Email _____

Personal Contact _____

Balance $ _____ Monthly Payment $ _____

Notes _____

Financial Institution _____

Card Type _____

Address _____

Associated Company _____

Website _____

Account No. _____

Card No. _____

Telephone _____ Email _____

Personal Contact _____

Balance $ _____ Monthly Payment $ _____

Notes _____

CREDIT ♦ CHARGE ♦ DEBIT ♦ ELECTRONIC PAYMENT

(AMEX, Apple Pay, Bank of America, Cash App, Chase, Discover, Google Pay, Mastercard, PayPal, Square, Venmo, Visa, Walmart, Wells Fargo, Zelle, Other...)

Financial Institution _____

Card Type _____

Address _____

Associated Company _____

Website _____

Account No. _____

Card No. _____

Telephone _____ Email _____

Personal Contact _____

Balance $ _____ Monthly Payment $ _____

Notes _____

Financial Institution _____

Card Type _____

Address _____

Associated Company _____

Website _____

Account No. _____

Card No. _____

Telephone _____ Email _____

Personal Contact _____

Balance $ _____ Monthly Payment $ _____

Notes _____

CREDIT ♦ CHARGE ♦ DEBIT ♦ ELECTRONIC PAYMENT

(AMEX, Apple Pay, Bank of America, Cash App, Chase, Discover, Google Pay, Mastercard, PayPal, Square, Venmo, Visa, Walmart, Wells Fargo, Zelle, Other...)

Financial Institution _____

Card Type _____

Address _____

Associated Company _____

Website _____

Account No. _____

Card No. _____

Telephone _____ Email _____

Personal Contact _____

Balance $ _____ Monthly Payment $ _____

Notes _____

Financial Institution _____

Card Type _____

Address _____

Associated Company _____

Website _____

Account No. _____

Card No. _____

Telephone _____ Email _____

Personal Contact _____

Balance $ _____ Monthly Payment $ _____

Notes _____

CREDIT ♦ CHARGE ♦ DEBIT ♦ ELECTRONIC PAYMENT

(AMEX, Apple Pay, Bank of America, Cash App, Chase, Discover, Google Pay, Mastercard, PayPal, Square, Venmo, Visa, Walmart, Wells Fargo, Zelle, Other...)

Financial Institution _____

Card Type _____

Address _____

Associated Company _____

Website _____

Account No. _____

Card No. _____

Telephone _____ Email _____

Personal Contact _____

Balance $ _____ Monthly Payment $ _____

Notes _____

Financial Institution _____

Card Type _____

Address _____

Associated Company _____

Website _____

Account No. _____

Card No. _____

Telephone _____ Email _____

Personal Contact _____

Balance $ _____ Monthly Payment $ _____

Notes _____

CRYPTO-CURRENCY

(Bitcoin, Ethereum, Binance Coin, Tether, Solana, Cardano, U.S. Dollar Coin, XRP, Terra, Polkadot, Dogecoin, Shiba Inu, Other...)

Currency Exchange _____

Currency Type _____

Wallet ☐ Coinbase ☐ Mycelium ☐ Ledger Nano X

☐ Trezor ☐ Exodus ☐ Black Wall Street

☐ Electrum ☐ eToro ☐ Other

Wallet Custodian _____

Website _____

Telephone_____ Email _____

Account # _____

Private Crypto Keys _____

_____

Present Value _____

Notes _____

CRYPTO-CURRENCY

(Bitcoin, Ethereum, Binance Coin, Tether, Solana, Cardano, U.S. Dollar Coin, XRP, Terra, Polkadot, Dogecoin, Shiba Inu, Other...)

Currency Exchange _____

Currency Type _____

Wallet ☐ Coinbase ☐ Mycelium ☐ Ledger Nano X
☐ Trezor ☐ Exodus ☐ Black Wall Street
☐ Electrum ☐ eToro ☐ Other

Wallet Custodian _____

Website _____

Telephone_____ Email _____

Account # _____

Private Crypto Keys _____

Present Value _____

Notes _____

Currency Exchange _____

Currency Type _____

Wallet ☐ Coinbase ☐ Mycelium ☐ Ledger Nano X
☐ Trezor ☐ Exodus ☐ Black Wall Street
☐ Electrum ☐ eToro ☐ Other

Wallet Custodian _____

Website _____

Telephone_____ Email _____

Account # _____

Private Crypto Keys _____

Present Value _____

Notes _____

CRYPTO-CURRENCY

(Bitcoin, Ethereum, Binance Coin, Tether, Solana, Cardano, U.S. Dollar Coin, XRP, Terra, Polkadot, Dogecoin, Shiba Inu, Other...)

Currency Exchange _____

Currency Type _____

Wallet ☐ Coinbase ☐ Mycelium ☐ Ledger Nano X

☐ Trezor ☐ Exodus ☐ Black Wall Street

☐ Electrum ☐ eToro ☐ Other

Wallet Custodian _____

Website _____

Telephone_____ Email _____

Account # _____

Private Crypto Keys _____

_____

Present Value _____

Notes _____

Currency Exchange _____

Currency Type _____

Wallet ☐ Coinbase ☐ Mycelium ☐ Ledger Nano X

☐ Trezor ☐ Exodus ☐ Black Wall Street

☐ Electrum ☐ eToro ☐ Other

Wallet Custodian _____

Website _____

Telephone_____ Email _____

Account # _____

Private Crypto Keys _____

_____

Present Value _____

Notes _____

CRYPTO-CURRENCY

(Bitcoin, Ethereum, Binance Coin, Tether, Solana, Cardano, U.S. Dollar Coin, XRP, Terra, Polkadot, Dogecoin, Shiba Inu, Other...)

Currency Exchange _____

Currency Type _____

Wallet ☐ Coinbase ☐ Mycelium ☐ Ledger Nano X
       ☐ Trezor ☐ Exodus ☐ Black Wall Street
       ☐ Electrum ☐ eToro ☐ Other

Wallet Custodian _____

Website _____

Telephone_____ Email _____

Account # _____

Private Crypto Keys _____

_____

Present Value _____

Notes _____

Currency Exchange _____

Currency Type _____

Wallet ☐ Coinbase ☐ Mycelium ☐ Ledger Nano X
       ☐ Trezor ☐ Exodus ☐ Black Wall Street
       ☐ Electrum ☐ eToro ☐ Other

Wallet Custodian _____

Website _____

Telephone_____ Email _____

Account # _____

Private Crypto Keys _____

_____

Present Value _____

Notes _____

CRYPTO-CURRENCY

(Bitcoin, Ethereum, Binance Coin, Tether, Solana, Cardano, U.S. Dollar Coin, XRP, Terra, Polkadot, Dogecoin, Shiba Inu, Other...)

Currency Exchange _____

Currency Type _____

Wallet ☐ Coinbase   ☐ Mycelium   ☐ Ledger Nano X

        ☐ Trezor   ☐ Exodus   ☐ Black Wall Street

        ☐ Electrum   ☐ eToro   ☐ Other

Wallet Custodian _____

Website _____

Telephone_____ Email _____

Account # _____

Private Crypto Keys _____

_____

Present Value _____

Notes _____

Currency Exchange _____

Currency Type _____

Wallet ☐ Coinbase   ☐ Mycelium   ☐ Ledger Nano X

        ☐ Trezor   ☐ Exodus   ☐ Black Wall Street

        ☐ Electrum   ☐ eToro   ☐ Other

Wallet Custodian _____

Website _____

Telephone_____ Email _____

Account # _____

Private Crypto Keys _____

_____

Present Value _____

Notes _____

CRYPTO-CURRENCY

(Bitcoin, Ethereum, Binance Coin, Tether, Solana, Cardano, U.S. Dollar Coin, XRP, Terra, Polkadot, Dogecoin, Shiba Inu, Other...)

Currency Exchange _____

Currency Type _____

Wallet ☐ Coinbase ☐ Mycelium ☐ Ledger Nano X
       ☐ Trezor ☐ Exodus ☐ Black Wall Street
       ☐ Electrum ☐ eToro ☐ Other

Wallet Custodian _____

Website _____

Telephone _____ Email _____

Account # _____

Private Crypto Keys _____

Present Value _____

Notes _____

Currency Exchange _____

Currency Type _____

Wallet ☐ Coinbase ☐ Mycelium ☐ Ledger Nano X
       ☐ Trezor ☐ Exodus ☐ Black Wall Street
       ☐ Electrum ☐ eToro ☐ Other

Wallet Custodian _____

Website _____

Telephone _____ Email _____

Account # _____

Private Crypto Keys _____

Present Value _____

Notes _____

CRYPTO-CURRENCY

(Bitcoin, Ethereum, Binance Coin, Tether, Solana, Cardano, U.S. Dollar Coin, XRP, Terra, Polkadot, Dogecoin, Shiba Inu, Other...)

Currency Exchange _____

Currency Type _____

Wallet ☐ Paper ☐ Hardware ☐ Onliner

Wallet Custodian _____

Website _____

Telephone_____ Email _____

Account # _____

Private Crypto Keys _____

_____

Present Value _____

Notes _____

Currency Exchange _____

Currency Type _____

Wallet ☐ Paper ☐ Hardware ☐ Onliner

Wallet Custodian _____

Website _____

Telephone_____ Email _____

Account # _____

Private Crypto Keys _____

_____

Present Value _____

Notes _____

CRYPTO-CURRENCY

*(Bitcoin, Ethereum, Binance Coin, Tether, Solana, Cardano, U.S. Dollar Coin,
XRP, Terra, Polkadot, Dogecoin, Shiba Inu, Other...)*

Currency Exchange _____

Currency Type _____

Wallet ☐ Paper   ☐ Hardware   ☐ Onliner

Wallet Custodian _____

Website _____

Telephone_____ Email _____

Account # _____

Private Crypto Keys _____

_____

Present Value _____

Notes _____

Currency Exchange _____

Currency Type _____

Wallet ☐ Paper   ☐ Hardware   ☐ Onliner

Wallet Custodian _____

Website _____

Telephone_____ Email _____

Account # _____

Private Crypto Keys _____

_____

Present Value _____

Notes _____

DEBTS

Company I Owe _____

Person I Owe _____

Name on Account _____

Account # _____

Telephone _____

Debt Amount $_____

Company I Owe _____

Person I Owe _____

Name on Account _____

Account # _____

Telephone _____

Debt Amount $_____

Company I Owe _____

Person I Owe _____

Name on Account _____

Account # _____

Telephone _____

Debt Amount $_____

Company I Owe _____

Person I Owe _____

Name on Account _____

Account # _____

Telephone _____

Debt Amount $ _____

Company I Owe _____

Person I Owe _____

Name on Account _____

Account # _____

Telephone _____

Debt Amount $ _____

Company I Owe _____

Person I Owe _____

Name on Account _____

Account # _____

Telephone _____

Debt Amount $ _____

Company I Owe _____

Person I Owe _____

Name on Account _____

Account # _____

Telephone _____

Debt Amount $ _____

Company I Owe _____

Person I Owe _____

Name on Account _____

Account # _____

Telephone _____

Debt Amount $ _____

FIREARMS, FISHING & HUNTING

Item _____

Location _____

Registration info _____

Permit info _____

Notes _____

Item _____

Location _____

Registration info _____

Permit info _____

Notes _____

Item _____

Location _____

Registration info _____

Permit info _____

Notes _____

Item _____

Location _____

Registration info _____

Permit info _____

Notes _____

Item _____

Location _____

Registration info _____

Permit info _____

Notes _____

Item _____

Location _____

Registration info _____

Permit info _____

Notes _____

Item _____

Location _____

Registration info _____

Permit info _____

Notes _____

Item _____

Location _____

Registration info _____

Permit info _____

Notes _____

HEIRLOOMS & OTHER VALUABLES

Item _____

Location _____

Instructions _____

Notes _____

_____

Item _____

Location _____

Instructions _____

Notes _____

_____

Item _____

Location _____

Instructions _____

Notes _____

_____

Item _____

Location _____

Instructions _____

Notes _____

_____

Item _____

Location _____

Instructions _____

Notes _____

Item _____

Location _____

Instructions _____

Notes _____

Item _____

Location _____

Instructions _____

Notes _____

Item _____

Location _____

Instructions _____

Notes _____

Item _____

Location _____

Instructions _____

Notes _____

Item _____

Location _____

Instructions _____

Notes _____

INSURANCE

(Airplane, Art, ATV, Auto, Boat, Condo, Contents, Golf Cart, Health, Jet Ski, Jewelry, Life, Renters, RV, Medicaid, Medicare, Motorcycle, Travel, Truck, Other...)

Insurance Type _____

Company _____ Policy Amount $ _____

Address _____

Policy No. _____ Expires _____

Annual Premium $ _____ Monthly Payment $ _____

Fund Name _____ Account No. _____

Share Price $ _____ Investment Amount $ _____

Date Opened _____ Date Closed _____

Agent _____

Website _____

Telephone _____ Email _____

Beneficiary _____

Roadside Assistance Company _____

Telephone _____ Website _____

Notes _____

INSURANCE

(Airplane, Art, ATV, Auto, Boat, Condo, Contents, Golf Cart, Health, Jet Ski, Jewelry, Life, Renters, RV, Medicaid, Medicare, Motorcycle, Travel, Truck, Other...)

Insurance Type _____

Company _____ Policy Amount $ _____

Address _____

Policy No. _____ Expires _____

Annual Premium $ _____ Monthly Payment $ _____

Fund Name _____ Account No. _____

Share Price $ _____ Investment Amount $ _____

Date Opened _____ Date Closed _____

Agent _____

Website _____

Telephone _____ Email _____

Beneficiary _____

Roadside Assistance Company _____

Telephone _____ Website _____

Notes _____

Insurance Type _____

Company _____ Policy Amount $ _____

Address _____

Policy No. _____ Expires _____

Annual Premium $ _____ Monthly Payment $ _____

Fund Name _____ Account No. _____

Share Price $ _____ Investment Amount $ _____

Date Opened _____ Date Closed _____

Agent _____

Website _____

Telephone _____ Email _____

Beneficiary _____

Roadside Assistance Company _____

Telephone _____ Website _____

Notes _____

INSURANCE
(Airplane, Art, ATV, Auto, Boat, Condo, Contents, Golf Cart, Health, Jet Ski, Jewelry, Life, Renters, RV, Medicaid, Medicare, Motorcycle, Travel, Truck, Other...)

Insurance Type _____

Company _____ Policy Amount $ _____

Address _____

Policy No. _____ Expires _____

Annual Premium $ _____ Monthly Payment $ _____

Fund Name _____ Account No. _____

Share Price $ _____ Investment Amount $ _____

Date Opened _____ Date Closed _____

Agent _____

Website _____

Telephone _____ Email _____

Beneficiary _____

Roadside Assistance Company _____

Telephone _____ Website _____

Notes _____

Insurance Type _____

Company _____ Policy Amount $ _____

Address _____

Policy No. _____ Expires _____

Annual Premium $ _____ Monthly Payment $ _____

Fund Name _____ Account No. _____

Share Price $ _____ Investment Amount $ _____

Date Opened _____ Date Closed _____

Agent _____

Website _____

Telephone _____ Email _____

Beneficiary _____

Roadside Assistance Company _____

Telephone _____ Website _____

Notes _____

INSURANCE

(Airplane, Art, ATV, Auto, Boat, Condo, Contents, Golf Cart, Health, Jet Ski, Jewelry, Life, Renters, RV, Medicaid, Medicare, Motorcycle, Travel, Truck, Other...)

Insurance Type _____

Company _____ Policy Amount $ _____

Address _____

Policy No. _____ Expires _____

Annual Premium $ _____ Monthly Payment $ _____

Fund Name _____ Account No. _____

Share Price $ _____ Investment Amount $ _____

Date Opened _____ Date Closed _____

Agent _____

Website _____

Telephone _____ Email _____

Beneficiary _____

Roadside Assistance Company _____

Telephone _____ Website _____

Notes _____

Insurance Type _____

Company _____ Policy Amount $ _____

Address _____

Policy No. _____ Expires _____

Annual Premium $ _____ Monthly Payment $ _____

Fund Name _____ Account No. _____

Share Price $ _____ Investment Amount $ _____

Date Opened _____ Date Closed _____

Agent _____

Website _____

Telephone _____ Email _____

Beneficiary _____

Roadside Assistance Company _____

Telephone _____ Website _____

Notes _____

INSURANCE

(Airplane, Art, ATV, Auto, Boat, Condo, Contents, Golf Cart, Health, Jet Ski, Jewelry, Life, Renters, RV, Medicaid, Medicare, Motorcycle, Travel, Truck, Other...)

Insurance Type _____

Company _____ Policy Amount $ _____

Address _____

Policy No. _____ Expires _____

Annual Premium $ _____ Monthly Payment $ _____

Fund Name _____ Account No. _____

Share Price $ _____ Investment Amount $ _____

Date Opened _____ Date Closed _____

Agent _____

Website _____

Telephone _____ Email _____

Beneficiary _____

Roadside Assistance Company _____

Telephone _____ Website _____

Notes _____

Insurance Type _____

Company _____ Policy Amount $ _____

Address _____

Policy No. _____ Expires _____

Annual Premium $ _____ Monthly Payment $ _____

Fund Name _____ Account No. _____

Share Price $ _____ Investment Amount $ _____

Date Opened _____ Date Closed _____

Agent _____

Website _____

Telephone _____ Email _____

Beneficiary _____

Roadside Assistance Company _____

Telephone _____ Website _____

Notes _____

INSURANCE

(Airplane, Art, ATV, Auto, Boat, Condo, Contents, Golf Cart, Health, Jet Ski, Jewelry, Life, Renters, RV, Medicaid, Medicare, Motorcycle, Travel, Truck, Other...)

Insurance Type _____

Company _____ Policy Amount $ _____

Address _____

Policy No. _____ Expires _____

Annual Premium $ _____ Monthly Payment $ _____

Fund Name _____ Account No. _____

Share Price $ _____ Investment Amount $ _____

Date Opened _____ Date Closed _____

Agent _____

Website _____

Telephone _____ Email _____

Beneficiary _____

Roadside Assistance Company _____

Telephone _____ Website _____

Notes _____

Insurance Type _____

Company _____ Policy Amount $ _____

Address _____

Policy No. _____ Expires _____

Annual Premium $ _____ Monthly Payment $ _____

Fund Name _____ Account No. _____

Share Price $ _____ Investment Amount $ _____

Date Opened _____ Date Closed _____

Agent _____

Website _____

Telephone _____ Email _____

Beneficiary _____

Roadside Assistance Company _____

Telephone _____ Website _____

Notes _____

INSURANCE

(Airplane, Art, ATV, Auto, Boat, Condo, Contents, Golf Cart, Health, Jet Ski, Jewelry, Life, Renters, RV, Medicaid, Medicare, Motorcycle, Travel, Truck, Other...)

Insurance Type _____

Company _____ Policy Amount $ _____

Address _____

Policy No. _____ Expires _____

Annual Premium $ _____ Monthly Payment $ _____

Fund Name _____ Account No. _____

Share Price $ _____ Investment Amount $ _____

Date Opened _____ Date Closed _____

Agent _____

Website _____

Telephone _____ Email _____

Beneficiary _____

Roadside Assistance Company _____

Telephone _____ Website _____

Notes _____

Insurance Type _____

Company _____ Policy Amount $ _____

Address _____

Policy No. _____ Expires _____

Annual Premium $ _____ Monthly Payment $ _____

Fund Name _____ Account No. _____

Share Price $ _____ Investment Amount $ _____

Date Opened _____ Date Closed _____

Agent _____

Website _____

Telephone _____ Email _____

Beneficiary _____

Roadside Assistance Company _____

Telephone _____ Website _____

Notes _____

INSURANCE
(Airplane, Art, ATV, Auto, Boat, Condo, Contents, Golf Cart, Health, Jet Ski, Jewelry, Life, Renters, RV, Medicaid, Medicare, Motorcycle, Travel, Truck, Other...)

Insurance Type _____

Company _____ Policy Amount $ _____

Address _____

Policy No. _____ Expires _____

Annual Premium $ _____ Monthly Payment $ _____

Fund Name _____ Account No. _____

Share Price $ _____ Investment Amount $ _____

Date Opened _____ Date Closed _____

Agent _____

Website _____

Telephone _____ Email _____

Beneficiary _____

Roadside Assistance Company _____

Telephone _____ Website _____

Notes _____

Insurance Type _____

Company _____ Policy Amount $ _____

Address _____

Policy No. _____ Expires _____

Annual Premium $ _____ Monthly Payment $ _____

Fund Name _____ Account No. _____

Share Price $ _____ Investment Amount $ _____

Date Opened _____ Date Closed _____

Agent _____

Website _____

Telephone _____ Email _____

Beneficiary _____

Roadside Assistance Company _____

Telephone _____ Website _____

Notes _____

INTERNET ♦ SOCIAL MEDIA ♦ EMAIL ♦ TV

(These accounts will need closing ...)

META (FACEBOOK)
Username _____
Password _____

TWITTER
Username _____
Password _____

INSTAGRAM
Username _____
Password _____

YOUTUBE
Username _____
Password _____

LINKEDIN
Username _____
Password _____

PINTEREST
Username _____
Password _____

TIK TOK
Username _____
Password _____

GOOGLE
Username _____
Password _____

REDDIT
Username _____
Password _____

APPLE ID
Username _____
Password _____

NETFLIX
Username _____
Password _____

HULU
Username _____
Password _____

AMAZON PRIME
Username _____
Password _____

DISNEY +
Username _____
Password _____

OTHER
Username _____
Password _____

EMAIL ADDRESS
Password _____

EMAIL ADDRESS
Password _____

EMAIL ADDRESS
Password _____

MONEY MARKET FUNDS

Financial Institution _____

Address _____

Representative _____

Website _____

Telephone _____ Email _____

Account No. _____

Interest Rate _____ Annual Yield _____

Initial Investmant _____

Present Value _____

Financial Institution _____

Address _____

Representative _____

Website _____

Telephone _____ Email _____

Account No. _____

Interest Rate _____ Annual Yield _____

Initial Investmant _____

Present Value _____

MONEY MARKET FUNDS

Financial Institution _____

Address _____

Representative _____

Website _____

Telephone _____ Email _____

Account No. _____

Interest Rate _____ Annual Yield _____

Initial Investmant _____

Present Value _____

Financial Institution _____

Address _____

Representative _____

Website _____

Telephone _____ Email _____

Account No. _____

Interest Rate _____ Annual Yield _____

Initial Investmant _____

Present Value _____

Financial Institution _____

Address _____

Representative _____

Website _____

Telephone _____ Email _____

Account No. _____

Interest Rate _____ Annual Yield _____

Initial Investmant _____

Present Value _____

MONEY MARKET FUNDS

Financial Institution _____

Address _____

Representative _____

Website _____

Telephone _____ Email _____

Account No. _____

Interest Rate _____ Annual Yield _____

Initial Investmant _____

Present Value _____

Financial Institution _____

Address _____

Representative _____

Website _____

Telephone _____ Email _____

Account No. _____

Interest Rate _____ Annual Yield _____

Initial Investmant _____

Present Value _____

Financial Institution _____

Address _____

Representative _____

Website _____

Telephone _____ Email _____

Account No. _____

Interest Rate _____ Annual Yield _____

Initial Investmant _____

Present Value _____

MONEY MARKET FUNDS

Financial Institution _____

Address _____

Representative _____

Website _____

Telephone _____ Email _____

Account No. _____

Interest Rate _____ Annual Yield _____

Initial Investmant _____

Present Value _____

Financial Institution _____

Address _____

Representative _____

Website _____

Telephone _____ Email _____

Account No. _____

Interest Rate _____ Annual Yield _____

Initial Investmant _____

Present Value _____

Financial Institution _____

Address _____

Representative _____

Website _____

Telephone _____ Email _____

Account No. _____

Interest Rate _____ Annual Yield _____

Initial Investmant _____

Present Value _____

MONEY MARKET FUNDS

Financial Institution _____

Address _____

Representative _____

Website _____

Telephone _____ Email _____

Account No. _____

Interest Rate _____ Annual Yield _____

Initial Investmant _____

Present Value _____

Financial Institution _____

Address _____

Representative _____

Website _____

Telephone _____ Email _____

Account No. _____

Interest Rate _____ Annual Yield _____

Initial Investmant _____

Present Value _____

Financial Institution _____

Address _____

Representative _____

Website _____

Telephone _____ Email _____

Account No. _____

Interest Rate _____ Annual Yield _____

Initial Investmant _____

Present Value _____

MONEY MARKET FUNDS

Financial Institution _____

Address _____

Representative _____

Website _____

Telephone _____ Email _____

Account No. _____

Interest Rate _____ Annual Yield _____

Initial Investmant _____

Present Value _____

Financial Institution _____

Address _____

Representative _____

Website _____

Telephone _____ Email _____

Account No. _____

Interest Rate _____ Annual Yield _____

Initial Investmant _____

Present Value _____

Financial Institution _____

Address _____

Representative _____

Website _____

Telephone _____ Email _____

Account No. _____

Interest Rate _____ Annual Yield _____

Initial Investmant _____

Present Value _____

MUTUAL FUNDS

Financial Institution _____

Address _____

Fund Name _____ Account No. _____

Share Price $ _____ Investment Amount $ _____

Date Opened _____ Date Closed _____

Representative _____

Website _____

Telephone _____ Email _____

Present Value $ _____

Notes _____

Financial Institution _____

Address _____

Fund Name _____ Account No. _____

Share Price $ _____ Investment Amount $ _____

Date Opened _____ Date Closed _____

Representative _____

Website _____

Telephone _____ Email _____

Present Value $ _____

Notes _____

MUTUAL FUNDS

Financial Institution _____
Address _____
Fund Name _____ Account No. _____
Share Price $ _____ Investment Amount $ _____
Date Opened _____ Date Closed _____
Representative _____
Website _____
Telephone _____ Email _____
Present Value $ _____
Notes _____

Financial Institution _____
Address _____
Fund Name _____ Account No. _____
Share Price $ _____ Investment Amount $ _____
Date Opened _____ Date Closed _____
Representative _____
Website _____
Telephone _____ Email _____
Present Value $ _____
Notes _____

Financial Institution _____
Address _____
Fund Name _____ Account No. _____
Share Price $ _____ Investment Amount $ _____
Date Opened _____ Date Closed _____
Representative _____
Website _____
Telephone _____ Email _____
Present Value $ _____
Notes _____

MUTUAL FUNDS

Financial Institution _____
Address _____
Fund Name _____ Account No. _____
Share Price $ _____ Investment Amount $ _____
Date Opened _____ Date Closed _____
Representative _____
Website _____
Telephone _____ Email _____
Present Value $ _____
Notes _____

Financial Institution _____
Address _____
Fund Name _____ Account No. _____
Share Price $ _____ Investment Amount $ _____
Date Opened _____ Date Closed _____
Representative _____
Website _____
Telephone _____ Email _____
Present Value $ _____
Notes _____

Financial Institution _____
Address _____
Fund Name _____ Account No. _____
Share Price $ _____ Investment Amount $ _____
Date Opened _____ Date Closed _____
Representative _____
Website _____
Telephone _____ Email _____
Present Value $ _____
Notes _____

MUTUAL FUNDS

Financial Institution _____
Address _____
Fund Name _____ Account No. _____
Share Price $ _____ Investment Amount $ _____
Date Opened _____ Date Closed _____
Representative _____
Website _____
Telephone _____ Email _____
Present Value $ _____
Notes _____

Financial Institution _____
Address _____
Fund Name _____ Account No. _____
Share Price $ _____ Investment Amount $ _____
Date Opened _____ Date Closed _____
Representative _____
Website _____
Telephone _____ Email _____
Present Value $ _____
Notes _____

Financial Institution _____
Address _____
Fund Name _____ Account No. _____
Share Price $ _____ Investment Amount $ _____
Date Opened _____ Date Closed _____
Representative _____
Website _____
Telephone _____ Email _____
Present Value $ _____
Notes _____

MUTUAL FUNDS

Financial Institution _____
Address _____
Fund Name _____ Account No. _____
Share Price $ _____ Investment Amount $ _____
Date Opened _____ Date Closed _____
Representative _____
Website _____
Telephone _____ Email _____
Present Value $ _____
Notes _____

Financial Institution _____
Address _____
Fund Name _____ Account No. _____
Share Price $ _____ Investment Amount $ _____
Date Opened _____ Date Closed _____
Representative _____
Website _____
Telephone _____ Email _____
Present Value $ _____
Notes _____

Financial Institution _____
Address _____
Fund Name _____ Account No. _____
Share Price $ _____ Investment Amount $ _____
Date Opened _____ Date Closed _____
Representative _____
Website _____
Telephone _____ Email _____
Present Value $ _____
Notes _____

MUTUAL FUNDS

Financial Institution _____
Address _____
Fund Name _____ Account No. _____
Share Price $ _____ Investment Amount $ _____
Date Opened _____ Date Closed _____
Representative _____
Website _____
Telephone _____ Email _____
Present Value $ _____
Notes _____

Financial Institution _____
Address _____
Fund Name _____ Account No. _____
Share Price $ _____ Investment Amount $ _____
Date Opened _____ Date Closed _____
Representative _____
Website _____
Telephone _____ Email _____
Present Value $ _____
Notes _____

Financial Institution _____
Address _____
Fund Name _____ Account No. _____
Share Price $ _____ Investment Amount $ _____
Date Opened _____ Date Closed _____
Representative _____
Website _____
Telephone _____ Email _____
Present Value $ _____
Notes _____

NON-FUNGIBLE TOKENS

Token Name _____

Crypto-Currency Used for Purchase _____

Currency Exchange _____

NFT Wallet ☐ Alpha Wallet ☐ Coin Base ☐ Math Wallet
           ☐ Metamask   ☐ Trust Wallet

Other _____

Website _____

Telephone _____ Account No _____

Crypto NFT Keys _____

_____

Purchase Value $ _____

Present Value $ _____

Sale Price _____

Notes _____

NON-FUNGIBLE TOKENS

Token Name _____

Crypto-Currency Used for Purchase _____

Currency Exchange _____

NFT Wallet ☐ Alpha Wallet ☐ Coin Base ☐ Math Wallet
☐ Metamask ☐ Trust Wallet

Other _____

Website _____

Telephone _____ Account No _____

Crypto NFT Keys _____

Purchase Value $ _____

Present Value $ _____

Sale Price _____

Notes _____

Token Name _____

Crypto-Currency Used for Purchase _____

Currency Exchange _____

NFT Wallet ☐ Alpha Wallet ☐ Coin Base ☐ Math Wallet
☐ Metamask ☐ Trust Wallet

Other _____

Website _____

Telephone _____ Account No _____

Crypto NFT Keys _____

Purchase Value $ _____

Present Value $ _____

Sale Price _____

Notes _____

NON-FUNGIBLE TOKENS

Token Name _____

Crypto-Currency Used for Purchase _____

Currency Exchange _____

NFT Wallet ☐ Alpha Wallet ☐ Coin Base ☐ Math Wallet
☐ Metamask ☐ Trust Wallet

Other _____

Website _____

Telephone _____ Account No _____

Crypto NFT Keys _____

_____

Purchase Value $ _____

Present Value $ _____

Sale Price _____

Notes _____

Token Name _____

Crypto-Currency Used for Purchase _____

Currency Exchange _____

NFT Wallet ☐ Alpha Wallet ☐ Coin Base ☐ Math Wallet
☐ Metamask ☐ Trust Wallet

Other _____

Website _____

Telephone _____ Account No _____

Crypto NFT Keys _____

_____

Purchase Value $ _____

Present Value $ _____

Sale Price _____

Notes _____

NON-FUNGIBLE TOKENS

Token Name _____

Crypto-Currency Used for Purchase _____

Currency Exchange _____

NFT Wallet ☐ Alpha Wallet ☐ Coin Base ☐ Math Wallet
            ☐ Metamask ☐ Trust Wallet

Other _____

Website _____

Telephone _____ Account No _____

Crypto NFT Keys _____

Purchase Value $ _____

Present Value $ _____

Sale Price _____

Notes _____

Token Name _____

Crypto-Currency Used for Purchase _____

Currency Exchange _____

NFT Wallet ☐ Alpha Wallet ☐ Coin Base ☐ Math Wallet
            ☐ Metamask ☐ Trust Wallet

Other _____

Website _____

Telephone _____ Account No _____

Crypto NFT Keys _____

Purchase Value $ _____

Present Value $ _____

Sale Price _____

Notes _____

NON-FUNGIBLE TOKENS

Token Name _____

Crypto-Currency Used for Purchase _____

Currency Exchange _____

NFT Wallet ☐ Alpha Wallet ☐ Coin Base ☐ Math Wallet
☐ Metamask ☐ Trust Wallet

Other _____

Website _____

Telephone _____ Account No _____

Crypto NFT Keys _____

Purchase Value $ _____

Present Value $ _____

Sale Price _____

Notes _____

Token Name _____

Crypto-Currency Used for Purchase _____

Currency Exchange _____

NFT Wallet ☐ Alpha Wallet ☐ Coin Base ☐ Math Wallet
☐ Metamask ☐ Trust Wallet

Other _____

Website _____

Telephone _____ Account No _____

Crypto NFT Keys _____

Purchase Value $ _____

Present Value $ _____

Sale Price _____

Notes _____

NON-FUNGIBLE TOKENS

Token Name _____

Crypto-Currency Used for Purchase _____

Currency Exchange _____

NFT Wallet ☐ Alpha Wallet ☐ Coin Base ☐ Math Wallet
             ☐ Metamask ☐ Trust Wallet

Other _____

Website _____

Telephone _____ Account No _____

Crypto NFT Keys _____

_____

Purchase Value $ _____

Present Value $ _____

Sale Price _____

Notes _____

Token Name _____

Crypto-Currency Used for Purchase _____

Currency Exchange _____

NFT Wallet ☐ Alpha Wallet ☐ Coin Base ☐ Math Wallet
             ☐ Metamask ☐ Trust Wallet

Other _____

Website _____

Telephone _____ Account No _____

Crypto NFT Keys _____

_____

Purchase Value $ _____

Present Value $ _____

Sale Price _____

Notes _____

PETS

Pet Name _____

Type of Pet _____ Breed _____

Home Address _____

Pet Sitter _____

Telephone _____ Email _____

Dog Walker _____

Telephone _____ Email _____

Veterinarian _____

Telephone _____ Email _____

Medications _____

Dietary Needs _____

Allergies _____

Microchip ☐ Yes ☐ No   Tracking Company _____

Inoculation Records Location _____

Emergency Contact _____

Telephone _____ Email _____

PETS

Pet Name _____
Type of Pet _____ Breed _____
Home Address _____
Pet Sitter _____
Telephone _____ Email _____
Dog Walker _____
Telephone _____ Email _____
Veterinarian _____
Telephone _____ Email _____
Medications _____
Dietary Needs _____
Allergies _____
Microchip [ ] Yes [ ] No   Tracking Company _____
Inoculation Records Location _____
Emergency Contact _____
Telephone _____ Email _____

Pet Name _____
Type of Pet _____ Breed _____
Home Address _____
Pet Sitter _____
Telephone _____ Email _____
Dog Walker _____
Telephone _____ Email _____
Veterinarian _____
Telephone _____ Email _____
Medications _____
Dietary Needs _____
Allergies _____
Microchip [ ] Yes [ ] No   Tracking Company _____
Inoculation Records Location _____
Emergency Contact _____
Telephone _____ Email _____

PETS

Pet Name _____

Type of Pet _____ Breed _____

Home Address _____

Pet Sitter _____

Telephone _____ Email _____

Dog Walker _____

Telephone _____ Email _____

Veterinarian _____

Telephone _____ Email _____

Medications _____

Dietary Needs _____

Allergies _____

Microchip ☐ Yes ☐ No   Tracking Company _____

Inoculation Records Location _____

Emergency Contact _____

Telephone _____ Email _____

Pet Name _____

Type of Pet _____ Breed _____

Home Address _____

Pet Sitter _____

Telephone _____ Email _____

Dog Walker _____

Telephone _____ Email _____

Veterinarian _____

Telephone _____ Email _____

Medications _____

Dietary Needs _____

Allergies _____

Microchip ☐ Yes ☐ No   Tracking Company _____

Inoculation Records Location _____

Emergency Contact _____

Telephone _____ Email _____

PETS

Pet Name —————————————————————————

Type of Pet ——————————— Breed ——————————

Home Address ————————————————————————

Pet Sitter —————————————————————————

Telephone ——————————— Email ——————————

Dog Walker —————————————————————————

Telephone ——————————— Email ——————————

Veterinarian ————————————————————————

Telephone ——————————— Email ——————————

Medications —————————————————————————

Dietary Needs ————————————————————————

Allergies ——————————————————————————

Microchip ☐ Yes ☐ No   Tracking Company —————————

Inoculation Records Location ——————————————————

Emergency Contact ————————————————————

Telephone ——————————— Email ——————————

Pet Name —————————————————————————

Type of Pet ——————————— Breed ——————————

Home Address ————————————————————————

Pet Sitter —————————————————————————

Telephone ——————————— Email ——————————

Dog Walker —————————————————————————

Telephone ——————————— Email ——————————

Veterinarian ————————————————————————

Telephone ——————————— Email ——————————

Medications —————————————————————————

Dietary Needs ————————————————————————

Allergies ——————————————————————————

Microchip ☐ Yes ☐ No   Tracking Company —————————

Inoculation Records Location ——————————————————

Emergency Contact ————————————————————

Telephone ——————————— Email ——————————

PROFESSIONAL ADVISORS

ATTORNEY _____

Company _____

Address _____

Telephone _____ Email _____

Website _____ Fax _____

TRUSTEE OF ESTATE _____

Company _____

Address _____

Telephone _____ Email _____

Website _____ Fax _____

EXECUTOR OF WILL _____

Company _____

Address _____

Telephone _____ Email _____

Website _____ Fax _____

POWER OF ATTORNEY _____

Company _____

Address _____

Telephone _____ Email _____

Website _____ Fax _____

CPA _____

Company _____

Address _____

Telephone _____ Email _____

Website _____ Fax _____

FINANCIAL PLANNER

Company _____

Address _____

Telephone _____ Email _____

Website _____ Fax _____

BOOKEEPER

Company _____

Address _____

Telephone _____ Email _____

Website _____ Fax _____

NOTARY PUBLIC

Company _____

Address _____

Telephone _____ Email _____

Website _____

HUMAN RESOURCE OFFICER

Company _____

Address _____

Telephone _____ Email _____

Website _____ Fax _____

FINANCIAL ADVISOR

Company _____

Address _____

Telephone _____ Email _____

Website _____ Fax _____

TAX PREPARER

Company _____

Address _____

Telephone _____ Email _____

Website _____ Fax _____

PROFFESSIONAL ADVISORS

ATTORNEY _____

Company _____

Address _____

Telephone _____ Email _____

Website _____ Fax _____

TRUSTEE OF ESTATE _____

Company _____

Address _____

Telephone _____ Email _____

Website _____ Fax _____

EXECUTOR OF WILL _____

Company _____

Address _____

Telephone _____ Email _____

Website _____ Fax _____

POWER OF ATTORNEY _____

Company _____

Address _____

Telephone _____ Email _____

Website _____ Fax _____

CPA _____

Company _____

Address _____

Telephone _____ Email _____

Website _____ Fax _____

FINANCIAL PLANNER _____

Company _____

Address _____

Telephone _____ Email _____

Website _____ Fax _____

BOOKEEPER

Company _____

Address _____

Telephone _____ Email _____

Website _____ Fax _____

NOTARY PUBLIC

Company _____

Address _____

Telephone _____ Email _____

Website _____

HUMAN RESOURCE OFFICER

Company _____

Address _____

Telephone _____ Email _____

Website _____ Fax _____

FINANCIAL ADVISOR

Company _____

Address _____

Telephone _____ Email _____

Website _____ Fax _____

TAX PREPARER

Company _____

Address _____

Telephone _____ Email _____

Website _____ Fax _____

REAL ESTATE

(Home, Investment, Lease, Rental, Airbnb, Vrbo, Timeshare, Other...)

Property Location _____

Type of Property _____
Broker _____
Telephone _____ Email _____
Purchase Price $ _____ Sale Price $ _____
Deed in name of _____

Deed Location _____

Mortgage $ _____
Mortgage Type _____
Monthly Payment $ _____
Bank / Lender _____
Address _____
Telephone _____ Email _____
Website _____
Assessed Value $ _____ Assessed Taxes $ _____
Payable To _____
Property Leased To _____
Address _____

Telephone _____ Email _____

Website _____

Referred by _____

Lease Start _____ Ends _____

Gross Income $ _____ Net $ _____

Insured by _____

Agent _____

Address _____

Telephone _____ Email _____

Website _____

Time Share Company _____

Initial Fee $ _____

Monthly Maintenance Fee $ _____

Annual Maintenance Fee $ _____

PROPERTY NOTES AND REAL ESTATE IMPROVEMENTS
(Home, Investment, Rental, Airbnb, Vrbo, Timeshares, Other...)

_____

_____

_____

_____

_____

_____

_____

REAL ESTATE

(Home, Investment, Rental, Airbnb, Vrbo, Timeshares, Other...)

Property Location _____

_____

Type of Property _____
Broker _____
Telephone _____ Email _____
Purchase Price $ _____ Sale Price $ _____
Deed in name of _____

_____

Deed Location _____

_____

Mortgage $ _____
Mortgage Type _____
Monthly Payment $ _____
Bank / Lender _____
Address _____
Telephone _____ Email _____
Website _____
Assessed Value $ _____ Assessed Taxes $ _____
Payable To _____
Property Leased To _____
Address _____
Telephone _____ Email _____
Website _____
Referred by _____
Lease Start _____ Ends _____
Gross Income $ _____ Net $ _____
Insured by _____

Agent _____

Address _____

Telephone _____ Email _____

Website _____

Time Share Company _____

Initial Fee $ _____

Monthly Maintenance Fee $ _____

Annual Maintenance Fee $ _____

PROPERTY NOTES AND REAL ESTATE IMPROVEMENTS

(Home, Investment, Rental, Airbnb, Vrbo, Timeshares, Other...)

_____

_____

_____

_____

_____

_____

_____

_____

_____

_____

_____

_____

REAL ESTATE

(Home, Investment, Rental, Airbnb, Vrbo, Timeshares, Other...)

Property Location _____

_____

Type of Property _____

Broker _____

Telephone _____ Email _____

Purchase Price $ _____ Sale Price $ _____

Deed in name of _____

_____

Deed Location _____

_____

Mortgage $ _____

Mortgage Type _____

Monthly Payment $ _____

Bank / Lender _____

Address _____

Telephone _____ Email _____

Website _____

Assessed Value $ _____ Assessed Taxes $ ____

Payable To _____

Property Leased To _____

Address _____

Telephone _____ Email _____

Website _____

Referred by _____

Lease Start _____ Ends _____

Gross Income $ _____ Net $ _____

Insured by _____

Agent _____

Address _____

Telephone _____ Email _____

Website _____

Time Share Company _____

Initial Fee $ _____

Monthly Maintenance Fee $ _____

Annual Maintenance Fee $ _____

PROPERTY NOTES AND REAL ESTATE IMPROVEMENTS

(Home, Investment, Rental, Airbnb, Vrbo, Timeshares, Other...)

_____

_____

_____

_____

_____

_____

_____

_____

_____

_____

_____

_____

_____

REAL ESTATE

(Home, Investment, Rental, Airbnb, Vrbo, Timeshares, Other...)

Property Location _____

_____

Type of Property _____
Broker _____
Telephone _____ Email _____
Purchase Price $ _____ Sale Price $ _____
Deed in name of _____

_____

Deed Location _____

_____

Mortgage $ _____
Mortgage Type _____
Monthly Payment $ _____
Bank / Lender _____
Address _____
Telephone _____ Email _____
Website _____
Assessed Value $ _____ Assessed Taxes $ _____
Payable To _____
Property Leased To _____
Address _____
Telephone _____ Email _____
Website _____
Referred by _____
Lease Start _____ Ends _____
Gross Income $ _____ Net $ _____
Insured by _____

Agent _____

Address _____

Telephone _____ Email _____

Website _____

Time Share Company _____

Initial Fee $ _____

Monthly Maintenance Fee $ _____

Annual Maintenance Fee $ _____

PROPERTY NOTES AND REAL ESTATE IMPROVEMENTS
(Home, Investment, Rental, Airbnb, Vrbo, Timeshares, Other...)

_____

_____

_____

_____

_____

_____

_____

_____

_____

_____

_____

_____

_____

_____

REAL ESTATE

(Home, Investment, Rental, Airbnb, Vrbo, Timeshares, Other...)

Property Location _____

_____

Type of Property _____

Broker _____

Telephone _____ Email _____

Purchase Price $ _____ Sale Price $ _____

Deed in name of _____

_____

Deed Location _____

_____

Mortgage $ _____

Mortgage Type _____

Monthly Payment $ _____

Bank / Lender _____

Address _____

Telephone _____ Email _____

Website _____

Assessed Value $ _____ Assessed Taxes $ _____

Payable To _____

Property Leased To _____

Address _____

Telephone _____ Email _____

Website _____

Referred by _____

Lease Start _____ Ends _____

Gross Income $ _____ Net $ _____

Insured by _____

Agent _____

Address _____

Telephone _____ Email _____

Website _____

Time Share Company _____

Initial Fee $ _____

Monthly Maintenance Fee $ _____

Annual Maintenance Fee $ _____

PROPERTY NOTES AND REAL ESTATE IMPROVEMENTS

(Home, Investment, Rental, Airbnb, Vrbo, Timeshares, Other...)

_____

_____

_____

_____

_____

_____

_____

_____

_____

_____

_____

_____

REAL ESTATE

(Home, Investment, Rental, Airbnb, Vrbo, Timeshares, Other...)

Property Location _____

_____

Type of Property _____

Broker _____

Telephone _____ Email _____

Purchase Price $ _____ Sale Price $ _____

Deed in name of _____

_____

Deed Location _____

_____

Mortgage $ _____

Mortgage Type _____

Monthly Payment $ _____

Bank / Lender _____

Address _____

Telephone _____ Email _____

Website _____

Assessed Value $ _____ Assessed Taxes $ _____

Payable To _____

Property Leased To _____

Address _____

Telephone _____ Email _____

Website _____

Referred by _____

Lease Start _____ Ends _____

Gross Income $ _____ Net $ _____

Insured by _____

Agent _____

Address _____

Telephone _____ Email _____

Website _____

Time Share Company _____

Initial Fee $ _____

Monthly Maintenance Fee $ _____

Annual Maintenance Fee $ _____

PROPERTY NOTES AND REAL ESTATE IMPROVEMENTS
(Home, Investment, Rental, Airbnb, Vrbo, Timeshares, Other...)

_____

_____

_____

_____

_____

_____

_____

_____

_____

_____

_____

_____

_____

_____

SAFE DEPOSIT BOX

Financial Institution _____

Address _____

Box _____ Date Rented _____

Those having access to box

Owner _____

Co-owner _____

Deputy _____

Other _____

Location of keys _____

STORAGE RECORD FOR VALUABLE PERSONAL POSSESSIONS

DATE STORED	
	Wills
	Marriage/Divorce/Birth/Death Certificates
	Military/Citizenship Documents
	Annuity Contracts
	Deeds
	Securities/Stocks/Bonds
	Insurance Documents
	Other

OTHER VALUABLE POSSESIONS

DATE STORED	
	Cash, Coins, Jewelry, Gems, Other…
	Other Personal Possessions

SAFE DEPOSIT BOX

Financial Institution _____

Address _____

Box _____ Date Rented _____

Those having access to box

Owner _____

Co-owner _____

Deputy _____

Other _____

Location of keys _____

OTHER VALUABLE POSSESSIONS

DATE STORED	
	Wills
	Marriage/Divorce/Birth/Death Certificates
	Military/Citizenship Documents
	Annuity Contracts
	Deeds
	Securities/Stocks/Bonds
	Insurance Documents
	Other

OTHER VALUABLE POSSESIONS

DATE STORED	
	Cash, Coins, Jewelry, Gems, Other…
	Other Personal Possessions

SAVINGS BONDS

DATE	SERIAL #	COST	MATURITY VALUE	MATURITY DATE

SAVINGS BONDS

DATE	SERIAL #	COST	MATURITY VALUE	MATURITY DATE

TRAVEL & OTHER REWARD PROGRAMS

Company _____

Name on Account _____

Account # _____

Telephone _____

Company _____

Name on Account _____

Account # _____

Telephone _____

Company _____

Name on Account _____

Account # _____

Telephone _____

Company _____

Name on Account _____

Account # _____

Telephone _____

Company _____

Name on Account _____

Account # _____

Telephone _____

Company _____

Name on Account _____

Account # _____

Telephone _____

Company _____

Name on Account _____

Account # _____

Telephone _____

Company _____

Name on Account _____

Account # _____

Telephone _____

Company _____

Name on Account _____

Account # _____

Telephone _____

Company _____

Name on Account _____

Account # _____

Telephone _____

Company _____

Name on Account _____

Account # _____

Telephone _____

TREASURY BILLS, NOTES & BONDS

Financial Institution _____

Address _____

Representative _____

Website _____

Telephone _____ Email _____

Account No _____

Purchase Date _____ Maturity Date _____

Term Length _____

Purchase Amount $ _____

Par Value $ _____

Financial Institution _____

Address _____

Representative _____

Website _____

Telephone _____ Email _____

Account No _____

Purchase Date _____ Maturity Date _____

Term Length _____

Purchase Amount $ _____

Par Value $ _____

TREASURY BILLS, NOTES & BONDS

Financial Institution _____

Address _____

Representative _____

Website _____

Telephone _____ Email _____

Account No _____

Purchase Date _____ Maturity Date _____

Term Length _____

Purchase Amount $ _____

Par Value $ _____

Financial Institution _____

Address _____

Representative _____

Website _____

Telephone _____ Email _____

Account No _____

Purchase Date _____ Maturity Date _____

Term Length _____

Purchase Amount $ _____

Par Value $ _____

Financial Institution _____

Address _____

Representative _____

Website _____

Telephone _____ Email _____

Account No _____

Purchase Date _____ Maturity Date _____

Term Length _____

Purchase Amount $ _____

Par Value $ _____

TREASURY BILLS, NOTES & BONDS

Financial Institution _____

Address _____

Representative _____

Website _____

Telephone _____ Email _____

Account No _____

Purchase Date _____ Maturity Date _____

Term Length _____

Purchase Amount $ _____

Par Value $ _____

Financial Institution _____

Address _____

Representative _____

Website _____

Telephone _____ Email _____

Account No _____

Purchase Date _____ Maturity Date _____

Term Length _____

Purchase Amount $ _____

Par Value $ _____

Financial Institution _____

Address _____

Representative _____

Website _____

Telephone _____ Email _____

Account No _____

Purchase Date _____ Maturity Date _____

Term Length _____

Purchase Amount $ _____

Par Value $ _____

TREASURY BILLS, NOTES & BONDS

Financial Institution _____

Address _____

Representative _____

Website _____

Telephone _____ Email _____

Account No _____

Purchase Date _____ Maturity Date _____

Term Length _____

Purchase Amount $ _____

Par Value $ _____

Financial Institution _____

Address _____

Representative _____

Website _____

Telephone _____ Email _____

Account No _____

Purchase Date _____ Maturity Date _____

Term Length _____

Purchase Amount $ _____

Par Value $ _____

Financial Institution _____

Address _____

Representative _____

Website _____

Telephone _____ Email _____

Account No _____

Purchase Date _____ Maturity Date _____

Term Length _____

Purchase Amount $ _____

Par Value $ _____

VEHICLES

(Airplane, ATV, Auto, Bicycle, Boat, Golf Cart, Jet Ski, Motorcycle, RV, Scooter, Truck, Other...)

Vehicle Type/Location _____

Make _____ Model _____

Key Location _____ Dealer _____

Title Holder _____ Monthly Payment $ _____

License Plate No. _____ VIN No. _____

Purchase Date _____ Amount $ _____

Sell Date _____ Amount $ _____

Insurance Company _____ Telephone _____

Roadside Assistance Co. _____ Telephone _____

Notes _____

Vehicle Type/Location _____

Make _____ Model _____

Key Location _____ Dealer _____

Title Holder _____ Monthly Payment $ _____

License Plate No. _____ VIN No. _____

Purchase Date _____ Amount $ _____

Sell Date _____ Amount $ _____

Insurance Company _____ Telephone _____

Roadside Assistance Co. _____ Telephone _____

Notes _____

VEHICLES

Vehicle Type/Location _____

Make _____ Model _____

Key Location _____ Dealer _____

Title Holder _____ Monthly Payment $ _____

License Plate No. _____ VIN No. _____

Purchase Date _____ Amount $ _____

Sell Date _____ Amount $ _____

Insurance Company _____ Telephone _____

Roadside Assistance Co. _____ Telephone _____

Notes _____

Vehicle Type/Location _____

Make _____ Model _____

Key Location _____ Dealer _____

Title Holder _____ Monthly Payment $ _____

License Plate No. _____ VIN No. _____

Purchase Date _____ Amount $ _____

Sell Date _____ Amount $ _____

Insurance Company _____ Telephone _____

Roadside Assistance Co. _____ Telephone _____

Notes _____

Vehicle Type/Location _____

Make _____ Model _____

Key Location _____ Dealer _____

Title Holder _____ Monthly Payment $ _____

License Plate No. _____ VIN No. _____

Purchase Date _____ Amount $ _____

Sell Date _____ Amount $ _____

Insurance Company _____ Telephone _____

Roadside Assistance Co. _____ Telephone _____

Notes _____

VEHICLES

Vehicle Type/Location _____

Make _____ Model _____

Key Location _____ Dealer _____

Title Holder _____ Monthly Payment $ _____

License Plate No. _____ VIN No. _____

Purchase Date _____ Amount $ _____

Sell Date _____ Amount $ _____

Insurance Company _____ Telephone _____

Roadside Assistance Co. _____ Telephone _____

Notes _____

Vehicle Type/Location _____

Make _____ Model _____

Key Location _____ Dealer _____

Title Holder _____ Monthly Payment $ _____

License Plate No. _____ VIN No. _____

Purchase Date _____ Amount $ _____

Sell Date _____ Amount $ _____

Insurance Company _____ Telephone _____

Roadside Assistance Co. _____ Telephone _____

Notes _____

Vehicle Type/Location _____

Make _____ Model _____

Key Location _____ Dealer _____

Title Holder _____ Monthly Payment $ _____

License Plate No. _____ VIN No. _____

Purchase Date _____ Amount $ _____

Sell Date _____ Amount $ _____

Insurance Company _____ Telephone _____

Roadside Assistance Co. _____ Telephone _____

Notes _____

VEHICLES

Vehicle Type Location _____
Make _____ Model _____
Key Location _____ Dealer _____
Title Holder _____ Monthly Payment $ _____
License Plate No. _____ VIN No. _____
Purchase Date _____ Amount $ _____
Sell Date _____ Amount $ _____
Insurance Company _____ Telephone _____
Roadside Assistance Co. _____ Telephone _____
Notes _____

Vehicle Type Location _____
Make _____ Model _____
Key Location _____ Dealer _____
Title Holder _____ Monthly Payment $ _____
License Plate No. _____ VIN No. _____
Purchase Date _____ Amount $ _____
Sell Date _____ Amount $ _____
Insurance Company _____ Telephone _____
Roadside Assistance Co. _____ Telephone _____
Notes _____

Vehicle Type Location _____
Make _____ Model _____
Key Location _____ Dealer _____
Title Holder _____ Monthly Payment $ _____
License Plate No. _____ VIN No. _____
Purchase Date _____ Amount $ _____
Sell Date _____ Amount $ _____
Insurance Company _____ Telephone _____
Roadside Assistance Co. _____ Telephone _____
Notes _____

OTHER IMPORTANT INFORMATION

PERSONAL NOTES & REFLECTIONS

Made in the USA
Monee, IL
06 March 2023

29301572R00070